DO YOU HAVE A BUSINESS NAME?

THERE IS A LOT THAT GOES INTO A NAME! MAKE SURE YOUR BUSINESS NAME CAN BE TRADEMARKED, DOESN'T INCLUDE ANY HIGH-RISK INDUSTRIES AND CAN BE OR IS FILED WITH THE STATE BEFORE YOU BUILD YOUR BUSINESS FURTHER.

DO YOU HAVE A BUSINESS ADDRESS?

- THE BUSINESS ADDRESS SHOULD NOT BE A VIRTUAL OR HOME ADDRESS.
- THE BUSINESS SHOULDN'T USE ANY TYPE OF PO BOX AS THE PHYSICAL ADDRESS. LENDERS TYPICALLY VIEW THIS TYPE OF ADDRESS AS HIGHER RISK.
- THE BUSINESS ADDRESS SHOULD BE USED ON ALL BUSINESS RECORDS.
- THE BUSINESS CAN USE A RESIDENTIAL ADDRESS AS THE BUSINESS ADDRESS.

ESTABLISH A BUSINESS ADDRESS

It's important for a business to have a business address.

In order to have a strong business foundation, your business should use a physical business address. Most lenders prefer that you have a business address but, you can use your residential address.

Do NOT use any type of PO Box for your business address. Many lenders see this as a higher risk business address.

What's most important is that your business address shows the same on ALL business records.

DO YOU HAVE A BUSINESS ENTITY?
GO ON THE SBA SITE AND REGISTER

- LLC/LLP
- PARTNERSHIP
- SOLE PROPRIETOR
- NON PROFIT

QUESTION TO ASK YOURSELF

ON YOUR BUSINESS ENTITY DOCUMENTS, IS THE BUSINESS ADDRESS AND OWNERSHIP CORRECT?

IS YOUR BUSINESS ADDRESS IN THE SAME STATE YOUR ENTITY IS FILED?

FILE YOUR BUSINESS ENTITY
IT'S IMPORTANT THAT YOU HAVE A STRONG BUSINESS FOUNDATION AND IT ALL STARTS WITH FILING YOUR BUSINESS ENTITY WITH YOUR SECRETARY OF STATE. EACH STATE HAS A DIFFERENT FILING AND FEE STRUCTURE. LIKE A BIRTH CERTIFICATE IS TO AN INDIVIDUAL A BUSINESS ENTITY IS THE BIRTH OF A BUSINESS.

DO YOU HAVE An EIN#

APPLY FOR YOUR BUSINESS'S EIN#
THE UNITED STATES REQUIRES ALL BUSINESS
ENTITIES TO FILE FOR AN EIN#. LIKE A SOCIAL
SECURITY NUMBER IS TO AN INDIVIDUAL AN EIN# IS
TO A BUSINESS.
HTTPS://WWW.IRS.GOV/BUSINESSES/SMALL-
BUSINESSES-SELF-EMPLOYED/APPLY-FOR-AN-
EMPLOYER-IDENTIFICATION-NUMBER-EIN-ONLINE

DO YOU HAVE A BUSINESS PHONE NUMBER?

WHAT IS IMPORTANT WHEN IT COMES TO YOUR BUSINESS PHONE?
DOES YOUR BUSINESS HAVE A PHONE NUMBER? CREDITORS PREFER TO SEE ACTUAL BUSINESS PHONE NUMBERS OPPOSED TO PERSONAL CELL PHONES OR RESIDENTIAL PHONES. IT'S IMPORTANT TO ALSO LIST YOUR BUSINESS PHONE NUMBER IN THE NATIONAL 411 DIRECTORY. KEEP IN MIND THAT UNFORTUNATELY CELL PHONE NUMBERS CAN'T BE LISTED IN THE NATIONAL 411 DIRECTORY.

SOME VENDORS WILL CHECK TO MAKE SURE YOUR BUSINESS PHONE NUMBER IS LISTED IN THE NATIONAL 411 DIRECTORY AND IF NOT, THEY MIGHT CHOOSE TO DECLINE YOU FOR THE ACCOUNT. WE WANT YOU TO HAVE THE BEST SUCCESS SO THAT IS WHY WE WANTED TO INFORM YOU OF ALL THE ABOVE INFORMATION.

RESOURCES:
RING CENTRAL
PHONE.COM
VONAGE

DOES YOUR BUSINESS HAVE A WEBSITE AND EMAIL?

SET UP BUSINESS WEBSITE & EMAIL A BUSINESS WEBSITE CAN DRASTICALLY AFFECT YOUR GROWTH. CLIENTS AND LENDERS ARE LOOKING FOR YOUR BUSINESS ONLINE. WHAT MESSAGE ARE YOU SENDING ONLINE? DO YOU HAVE AN ESTABLISHED WEBSITE THAT PORTRAYS THE IMAGE YOU WANT?

FOR EXAMPLE: GEORGE@GMAIL.COM AS A BUSINESS EMAIL ADDRESS DOESN'T LOOK AS PROFESSIONAL AS GEORGE@MYBUSINESSNAME.COM.

HAVING A BUSINESS WEBSITE AND EMAIL CAN BUILD CREDIBILITY. THOUGH NOT REQUIRED WE RECOMMEND THAT YOU HAVE A BUSINESS WEBSITE AND EMAIL.

RESOURCES:
GODADDY
WEBPAZ
MY WEB CHEF
SQUARESPACE
GOOGLE APPS

DO YOU HAVE ALL REQUIRED BUSINESS LICENSES?

GET YOUR REQUIRED BUSINESS LICENSES

Every city, state and county within the United States has different licensing requirements. Make sure you have all the required licenses.

DO YOU HAVE A BUSINESS BANK ACCOUNT?

SET UP YOUR BUSINESS BANK ACCOUNT

ALL BUSINESSES BIG OR SMALL, NEW OR ESTABLISHED SHOULD SET UP A BUSINESS BANK ACCOUNT. A BUSINESS BANK ACCOUNT OPENS UP FINANCING OPTIONS. ADDITIONALLY, A BUSINESS BANK ACCOUNT AFFECTS THE BUSINESS IN BOTH ACCOUNTING AND LEGAL DEPARTMENTS.

DO YOU HAVE BUSINESS MERCHANT ACCOUNT?

MERCHANT ACCOUNT

A MERCHANT ACCOUNTS ALLOWS YOUR BUSINESS TO ACCEPT CREDIT CARDS AND DEBIT CARDS. STATISTICALLY CUSTOMERS WILL SPEND MORE IF THEY CAN PURCHASE BY CARD. MERCHANT PROCESSING UNDER YOUR BUSINESS NAME ALSO INCREASES YOUR FINANCE OPTIONS.

RESOURCES:
PLATPAY
CAPITOL MERCHANT SOLUTIONS
SQUARE

DO ALL BUSINESS RECORDS LIST THE CORRECT BUSINESS NAME, ADDRESS, OWNERSHIP AND CONTACT INFORMATION?

DOES YOUR BUSINESS HAVE A DUNS # WITH DUN & BRADSTREET?

ESTABLISH YOUR DUNS

DUN & BRADSTREET IS ONE OF THE BUSINESS CREDIT BUREAUS. YOUR BUSINESS'S PROFILE IS SET UP WITH DUN & BRADSTREET WHEN YOU APPLY FOR A DUNS NUMBER, WHICH IN TURN ALLOWS TRADE ACCOUNTS YOU ESTABLISH THAT SHOULD REPORT TO DUN & BRADSTREET TO REPORT.

VERY IMPORTANT WHEN APPLYING FOR YOUR DUNS NUMBER TO USE THE EXACT SAME COMPANY NAME AND BUSINESS ADDRESS AS THE SECRETARY OF STATE AND IRS. CREDITORS WILL CHECK THE BUSINESS INFORMATION ON YOUR REPORT AGAINST PUBLIC RECORD. IF THERE ARE ANY VARIANCES, IT CAN LEAD TO A DECLINE.

DOES YOUR BUSINESS HAVE A PROFILE WITH BUSINESS EXPERIAN YET?

SEE IF YOUR COMPANY IS LISTED WITH EXPERIAN.

https://www.smartbusinessreports.com/ExperianBIN/

DOES YOUR BUSINESS HAVE A PROFILE WITH BUSINESS EQUIFAX YET?

SEE IF YOUR BUSINESS HAS A BUSINESS EQUIFAX REPORT IF YOU ARE UNSURE NO NEED TO WORRY, YOU CAN CALL EQUIFAX 888-407-0359 (CHOOSE OPTION 2, 2, THEN 4). THEY WILL ASK YOU FOR YOUR EIN NUMBER, BUSINESS NAME AND BUSINESS ADDRESS THEN THEY ARE GOING TO SEND BY MAIL THE BUSINESS CREDIT REPORT AND IT SHOULD BE RECEIVED WITHIN 7-10 BUSINESS DAYS. IF YOUR COMPANY HAS A PROFILE WITH BUSINESS EQUIFAX.

START BUILDING BUSINESS CREDIT

APPLY WITH 3 TRADE ACCOUNTS
WHAT IS A TRADE ACCOUNT? A TRADE ACCOUNT (SOMETIMES REFERRED TO AS A VENDOR ACCOUNT) IS TYPICALLY A STORE ACCOUNT. AS YOU SET UP YOUR ACCOUNTS WITH VARIOUS VENDORS MAKE SURE YOU ARE WORKING TOWARDS OR SETTING UP NET TERMS. PAYMENTS ON NET TERMS ARE REPORTED TO THE BUSINESS CREDIT BUREAUS.
WHEN APPLYING FOR TRADE ACCOUNTS MAKE SURE YOU USE YOUR CORRECT BUSINESS INFORMATION AS IT MATCHES ON ALL OF YOUR BUSINESS RECORDS.

TO MAKE SURE YOUR VENDORS REPORT MAKE SURE YOU PURCHASE IS OVER $50. IT TYPICALLY TAKES 30-90 DAYS TO COMPLETE THIS STEP AND FOR YOUR PAYMENTS TO REPORT ON YOUR BUSINESS CREDIT REPORTS. CONTINUE TO SEARCH YOUR REPORTS REGULARLY SO YOU ARE AWARE WHEN THEY START REPORTING.

CHOOSE 3 ACCOUNTS TO OPEN

CREATIVE ANALYTICS
QUALIFYING FACTOR

RECOMMENDED

REPORTS TO:
EQUIFAX

TERMS: NET 30

PG / NO PG:
NO PERSONAL GUARANTEE REQUIRED

BREX
QUALIFYING FACTOR

RECOMMENDED

REPORTS TO:
D&B, EXPERIAN AND EQUIFAX

TERMS: NET DAILY

PG / NO PG:
NO PERSONAL GUARANTEE REQUIRED

ULINE
QUALIFYING FACTOR

RECOMMENDED

REPORTS TO:
D&B AND EXPERIAN

TERMS: NET 30

PG / NO PG:
NO PERSONAL GUARANTEE REQUIRED

DOCUMENT RENT
QUALIFYING FACTOR

RECOMMENDED

REPORTS TO:
D&B

TERMS: NET 30

PG / NO PG:
NO PERSONAL GUARANTEE REQUIRED

JJ GOLD
QUALIFYING FACTOR

RECOMMENDED

REPORTS TO:
D&B AND EQUIFAX

TERMS: NET 30

PG / NO PG:
NO PERSONAL GUARANTEE REQUIRED

76
QUALIFYING FACTOR

RECOMMENDED

REPORTS TO:
D&B, EXPERIAN AND EQUIFAX

TERMS: NET 15

PG / NO PG:
PERSONAL GUARANTEE REQUIRED

MURPHY USA
Qualifying Factor

RECOMMENDED

REPORTS TO:
D&B, Experian, and Equifax

TERMS: Net 15

PG / NO PG:
Personal Guarantee Required

KUM & GO
Qualifying Factor

Based on your completion of the prior step this trade account has been unlocked
RECOMMENDED

REPORTS TO:
D&B, Experian, and Equifax

TERMS: Net 15

PG / NO PG:
Personal Guarantee Required

THE CEO CREATIVE
Qualifying Factor

RECOMMENDED

REPORTS TO:
Equifax

TERMS: Net 30

PG / NO PG:
No Personal Guarantee Required

ECREDABLE
Qualifying Factor

RECOMMENDED

REPORTS TO:
D&B AND EXPERIAN AND EQUIFAX

TERMS: NET 30

PG / NO PG:
NO PERSONAL GUARANTEE REQUIRED

WEX FLEET
Qualifying Factor

RECOMMENDED

REPORTS TO:
D&B, EXPERIAN, AND EQUIFAX

TERMS: NET 15, 22 OR REVOLVING

PG / NO PG:
PERSONAL GUARANTEE REQUIRED

GRAINGER INDUSTRIAL SUPPLY
Qualifying Factor

RECOMMENDED

REPORTS TO:
D&B

TERMS: NET 30

PG / NO PG:
NO PERSONAL GUARANTEE REQUIRED

ADVANCE AUTO PARTS
QUALIFYING FACTOR

RECOMMENDED

REPORTS TO:
D&B

TERMS: NET 7 OR 30

PG / NO PG:
NO PERSONAL GUARANTEE REQUIRED

CREDIT STRONG
QUALIFYING FACTOR

BASED ON YOUR COMPLETION OF THE PRIOR STEP THIS
TRADE ACCOUNT HAS BEEN UNLOCKED
RECOMMENDED

REPORTS TO:
EQUIFAX

TERMS: LOAN

PG / NO PG:
NO PERSONAL GUARANTEE REQUIRED

FULTON BANK
QUALIFYING FACTOR

RECOMMENDED

REPORTS TO:
D&B

TERMS: REVOLVING

PG / NO PG:
PERSONAL GUARANTEE REQUIRED

FLYING J
Qualifying Factor

RECOMMENDED

REPORTS TO:
D&B

TERMS: NET 1

PG / NO PG:
No Personal Guarantee Required

GENERAL MOTORS
Qualifying Factor

RECOMMENDED

REPORTS TO:
D&B

TERMS: Revolving

PG / NO PG:
Personal Guarantee Required

MARATHON
Qualifying Factor

RECOMMENDED

REPORTS TO:
D&B, Experian, and Equifax

TERMS: Net 15

PG / NO PG:
Personal Guarantee Required

APPLY FOR 3 MORE TRADE ACCOUNTS

YOU CURRENTLY HAVE AT LEAST 3 TRADE ACCOUNTS REPORTING, BUT NOW IT IS TIME TO ESTABLISH YOUR BUSINESS CREDIT REPORTS EVEN FURTHER. PLEASE SELECT AND APPLY FOR 3 MORE TRADE ACCOUNTS.

REMEMBER TO USE YOUR CORRECT BUSINESS INFORMATION WHEN APPLYING, AS ALL INFORMATION SHOULD MATCH YOUR BUSINESS RECORDS PERFECTLY.

WHEN YOU MAKE A PURCHASE, DO SO ON YOUR NET /CREDIT TERMS. IT IS PAYMENTS ON NET / CREDIT TERMS THAT ARE REPORTED.

IT TAKES 30-90 DAYS FROM THE DAY YOU MAKE YOUR PAYMENT FOR YOUR TRADE ACCOUNT TO REPORT ON YOUR BUSINESS CREDIT REPORT.

TA PETRO
QUALIFYING FACTOR

RECOMMENDED

REPORTS TO:
D&B, EXPERIAN, AND EQUIFAX

TERMS: NET 7 OR NET 30

PG / NO PG:
NO PERSONAL GUARANTEE REQUIRED

CEFCO
QUALIFYING FACTOR

BASED ON YOUR COMPLETION OF THE PRIOR STEP THIS
TRADE ACCOUNT HAS BEEN UNLOCKED
RECOMMENDED

REPORTS TO:
D&B, EXPERIAN AND EQUIFAX

TERMS: NET 7,NET 10,NET 14 OR NET 30

PG / NO PG:
NO PERSONAL GUARANTEE REQUIRED

NAMYNOT INC.
QUALIFYING FACTOR

RECOMMENDED

REPORTS TO:
D&B

TERMS: NET 30

PG / NO PG:
NO PERSONAL GUARANTEE REQUIRED

UNITED RENTALS
Qualifying Factor

RECOMMENDED

REPORTS TO:
Equifax

TERMS: Net 30, 45

PG / NO PG:
No Personal Guarantee Required

OFFICE DEPOT
Qualifying Factor

Based on your completion of the prior step this trade account
has been unlocked
RECOMMENDED

REPORTS TO:
D&B, Experian and Equifax

TERMS: Net 30, Net 60, or Revolving

PG / NO PG:
No Personal Guarantee Required

GLOBAL FLEET
Qualifying Factor

RECOMMENDED

REPORTS TO:
D&B, Experian and Equifax

TERMS: Net 30 or Revolving

PG / NO PG:
No Personal Guarantee Required

EXXON MOBIL
Qualifying Factor

RECOMMENDED

REPORTS TO:
D&B, Experian, and Equifax

TERMS: Net 15 or Revolving

PG / NO PG:
Personal Guarantee Required

HOME DEPOT
Qualifying Factor

RECOMMENDED

REPORTS TO:
D&B, Experian and Equifax

TERMS: Net 30, 60 or Revolving

PG / NO PG:
No Personal Guarantee Required

QUIK TRIP
Qualifying Factor

RECOMMENDED

REPORTS TO:
D&B, Experian, and Equifax

TERMS: Net 15

PG / NO PG:
Personal Guarantee Required

VALVOLINE FLEET
QUALIFYING FACTOR

RECOMMENDED

REPORTS TO:
D&B, EXPERIAN, AND EQUIFAX

TERMS: NET 15

PG / NO PG:
PERSONAL GUARANTEE REQUIRED

VALERO
QUALIFYING FACTOR

BASED ON YOUR COMPLETION OF THE PRIOR STEP THIS
TRADE ACCOUNT HAS BEEN UNLOCKED
RECOMMENDED

REPORTS TO:
D&B, EXPERIAN, AND EQUIFAX

TERMS: NET 15 OR REVOLVING

PG / NO PG:
PERSONAL GUARANTEE REQUIRED

LOWE'S HARDWARE
QUALIFYING FACTOR

RECOMMENDED

REPORTS TO:
D&B AND EXPERIAN

TERMS: NET 25, 30, OR 60

PG / NO PG:
NO PERSONAL GUARANTEE REQUIRED

APPLY FOR 3 TRADE ACCOUNTS

YOU CURRENTLY HAVE AT LEAST 6 TRADE ACCOUNTS REPORTING, BUT NOW IT IS TIME TO ESTABLISH YOUR BUSINESS CREDIT REPORTS EVEN FURTHER. PLEASE SELECT AND APPLY FOR 3 MORE TRADE ACCOUNTS.

REMEMBER TO USE YOUR CORRECT BUSINESS INFORMATION WHEN APPLYING, AS ALL INFORMATION SHOULD MATCH YOUR BUSINESS RECORDS PERFECTLY.

WHEN YOU MAKE A PURCHASE, DO SO ON YOUR NET /CREDIT TERMS. IT IS PAYMENTS ON NET / CREDIT TERMS THAT ARE REPORTED.

TO ENSURE THAT YOUR VENDOR'S REPORT YOUR PAYMENTS, MAKE A PURCHASE OF $50 OR MORE.

ON AVERAGE IT TAKES 30-90 DAYS FOR YOUR TRADE ACCOUNTS TO REPORT AND TO COMPLETE THIS STEP.

JETBLUE
Qualifying Factor

RECOMMENDED

REPORTS TO:
Experian and Equifax

TERMS: Revolving

PG / NO PG:
Personal Guarantee Required

GRAND + BENEDICTS
Qualifying Factor

RECOMMENDED

REPORTS TO:
D&B

TERMS: Net 30

PG / NO PG:
No Personal Guarantee Required

CLARK
Qualifying Factor

RECOMMENDED

REPORTS TO:
D&B, Experian and Equifax

TERMS: Net 15

PG / NO PG:
Personal Guarantee Required

CROWN OFFICE SUPPLIES
QUALIFYING FACTOR

RECOMMENDED

REPORTS TO:
D&B AND EQUIFAX

TERMS: NET 30

PG / NO PG:
NO PERSONAL GUARANTEE REQUIRED

RYDER
QUALIFYING FACTOR

BASED ON YOUR COMPLETION OF THE PRIOR STEP THIS
TRADE ACCOUNT HAS BEEN UNLOCKED
RECOMMENDED

REPORTS TO:
D&B, EXPERIAN AND EQUIFAX

TERMS: NET 7 OR 10

PG / NO PG:
NO PERSONAL GUARANTEE REQUIRED

CAPITAL ONTAP
QUALIFYING FACTOR

RECOMMENDED

REPORTS TO:
EXPERIAN

TERMS: REVOLVING

PG / NO PG:
PERSONAL GUARANTEE REQUIRED

SHELL
QUALIFYING FACTOR

RECOMMENDED

REPORTS TO:
D&B, EXPERIAN, AND EQUIFAX

TERMS: NET 22 OR REVOLVING

PG / NO PG:
PERSONAL GUARANTEE REQUIRED

SUMMA OFFICE SUPPLIES
QUALIFYING FACTOR

BASED ON YOUR COMPLETION OF THE PRIOR STEP THIS TRADE
ACCOUNT HAS BEEN UNLOCKED
RECOMMENDED

REPORTS TO:
EQUIFAX

TERMS: NET 30

PG / NO PG:
NO PERSONAL GUARANTEE REQUIRED

ROYAL FARMS
QUALIFYING FACTOR

RECOMMENDED

REPORTS TO:
D&B, EXPERIAN, AND EQUIFAX

TERMS: NET 15

PG / NO PG:
PERSONAL GUARANTEE REQUIRED

PLATT
QUALIFYING FACTOR

RECOMMENDED

REPORTS TO:
D&B AND EXPERIAN

TERMS: NET 30

PG / NO PG:
NO PERSONAL GUARANTEE REQUIRED

CITGO
QUALIFYING FACTOR

RECOMMENDED

REPORTS TO:
D&B, EXPERIAN AND EQUIFAX

TERMS: NET 15

PG / NO PG:
PERSONAL GUARANTEE REQUIRED

SPINX
QUALIFYING FACTOR

RECOMMENDED

REPORTS TO:
D&B, EXPERIAN, AND EQUIFAX

TERMS: NET 15

PG / NO PG:
PERSONAL GUARANTEE REQUIRED

UNIVERSAL PREMIUM
Qualifying Factor

RECOMMENDED

REPORTS TO:
D&B, Experian, and Equifax (can take up to 60-90 days
to report for the first payment to report)

TERMS: Net 7, 10, 13 or 15

PG / NO PG:
No Personal Guarantee Required

SAMS CLUB
Qualifying Factor

RECOMMENDED

REPORTS TO:
D&B

TERMS: Revolving

PG / NO PG:
No Personal Guarantee Required

PHILLIPS 66 / CONOCO / 76
COMMERCIAL
Qualifying Factor

RECOMMENDED

REPORTS TO:
D&B, Experian, and Equifax

TERMS: Net 15, Net 30 or Revolving

PG / NO PG:
Personal Guarantee Required

NOW ITS TIME FOR YOU TO GO APPLY FOR THE CAPITOL MONEY YOU NEED LOANS, CREDIT CARDS, ETC. GOOD LUCK IN YOUR BUSINESS

www.ingramcontent.com/pod-product-compliance
Lightning Source LLC
Chambersburg PA
CBHW040317010626
45792CB00023B/802